KATHRYN M. IRELAND
CLASSIC COUNTRY

KATHRYN M. IRELAND
CLASSIC COUNTRY

Gibbs Smith, Publisher
TO ENRICH AND INSPIRE HUMANKIND
Salt Lake City │ Charleston │ Santa Fe │ Santa Barbara

First Edition
11 10 09 08 07 5 4 3 2 1

Text © 2007 Kathryn M. Ireland
Photo credits on page 221

Published by
Gibbs Smith, Publisher
P.O. Box 667
Layton, Utah 84041

Orders: 1.800.835.4993
www.gibbs-smith.com

Designed by Debra McQuiston
Printed and bound in China

Library of Congress
Cataloging-in-Publication Data

Ireland, Kathryn M.
  Classic country / Kathryn M.
Ireland. — 1st ed.
     p. cm.
  ISBN-13: 978-1-4236-0168-5
  ISBN-10: 1-4236-0168-8
  1. Decoration and ornament,
Rustic. 2. Interior decoration.
I. Title.

NK1986.R8I75 2007
747—dc22

2007013286

To Berry, Joan, Nico,
who showed me the way.

CONTENTS

IT IS A MISTAKE to underestimate the significance of the relationship between humans and the cloth that they make. There is very little that is not revealed about the geography, status, economy, and above all identity of the maker or weaver of cloth; we are what wear and use cloth for. In modern, urban societies we have swapped natural or tribal costume for an adherence to the commands of international fashion houses. But the need to own or wear texture, colour, and pattern still results in the continuing reestablishment of our own identity.

FOREWORD

For those of us like Kathryn, who make and experiment with weaving and printing textiles for houses, we are merely continuing to try and satisfy the urge to unify comfort, ornament, pleasure and beauty.

Nothing is more fulfilling for us than to try and continue this perpetual tradition.

—Robert Kime

Oxenwood

23 March 2007

WHEN IT COMES to designing a room, my first point of reference is the fabric. For others it may be the artwork, the antiques or just simply the architecture. For me it's the combining of color and texture that brings a room to life.

From a young age, I was always crazy for color. I was the one in my family who insisted on wearing brightly colored clothes and changing the furniture around almost on a weekly basis. It wasn't just one color or one pattern that fascinated me, but how you put them together in a room. I realized early on that one could dictate the effect of the

INTRODUCTION

room simply by arranging the furniture and adding color. While most other girls my age were only interested in getting their outfits right, I was scheming colors and fabrics for my bedroom. Even though I grew up surrounded by the opulent architecture of London, I always felt most at home in the country. The time spent at our seaside cottage on the west coast of Scotland always made me the happiest. Waking up to the sound of the waves and the undulating green of the hills around us has made me at heart a country girl.

My mother, Lillian, gave me free range for decorating my bedroom, which I shared with my younger sister, Mary Jane. I painted it "Perrier green" and hung netting over my bed. I understood from that moment that fabric has the power to make one feel like a princess.

Having left school with A levels in English and textile design, I jumped headfirst into the wildness that was London in the eighties. I had jobs in journalism, fashion and public relations. By the age of twenty-two, I saw my life stretched out before me and could see that I was setting myself up for a long and successful career helping other creative people. This wasn't for me—I'm a creative person, and although I hadn't decided to be an interior designer, I knew that my life would be colorful in some way. On arriving in Los Angeles and falling in love with its sunny, breezy, bohemian lifestyle, I decided it would be my home. Within six weeks of arrival I met and married Gary, the father of my boys.

Gary's film editing studio soon became the home to my first little shop, where I turned my collection of antique fabric remnants into pillows and sold those along with my flea market finds. Retail stores selling great furnishings to the public, at the time, were a novelty. Coming from England, where you could throw together a house in a weekend, I found it very difficult to furnish a home in Los Angeles because the best shops were off-limits to nonprofessionals, and I certainly wasn't going to hire a decorator. What I realized later was that you do, in fact, need a professional to re-cover things, upholster and generally navigate the client through the process of doing a house. When I started out,

I was green and all of this was new to me. And through my own mistakes I learned the secrets to decorating.

Having always been fascinated with fabrics and having collected both antique and local fabrics on my travels, I have built a library of textiles over the years that includes Ghanian tribal cloth, rare weavings from Uzbekistan, embroidery from Pakistan and India, and pieces of wallpaper found in ramshackle houses—anything that caught my eye. My parents, like so many of their generation, were adamant that my brothers and sister and I were aware of the world. My mother had been brought up in Egypt and my father had traveled around the world at least once before his children were born; it was almost a requirement that I travel. As children, we spent our holidays cavorting from the lowlands of Scotland to the Mediterranean beaches, soaking up the local color. Little did I know that later in life, it would be these carefree times that would influence so much of how I approach my design process.

Interior design wasn't something that I hotly pursued, but I sometimes feel it pursued me. I had no formal design training but always was close to fabulously stylish, creative people. People and the places I traveled were my education.

It was while designing for friends that I realized I had my own fabric collection in me. I threw myself into my

piles of collected inspiration only to realize that I had my first six designs lying on top of me at night: my favorite nineteenth-century quilt that had remained intact until it arrived on my bed had fantastic coordination and color. With my boys using the mattress for their nightly rags, the quilt was falling into disarray. Taking some of its motifs and images for inspiration, I started to play around with scale.

I'm not sure how or when my appreciation of textiles came about. Maybe it was winning the needlework prize when I was seven with my patch-work quilt, or perhaps the Textile and Design course I took pre-college at school in London. Whatever the source of the fire, it wasn't until I was working full time with fabric that I realized I wanted to design my own line, and it seemed to me there was room in the market for my color palette and design ideas.

My first fabric collection was launched in the autumn of 1997. Our relationship to fabric, unlike our rela-tionship to any other material, is an intimate and special one. From the

dawn of humankind, we have worn cloth against our skin as protection, as armor, as decoration and as signifier. When I cover a couch or a wall or any surface with material, I take into account those who will live with it every day. Fabric is the most personal and human of all the materials we use in interior design and architecture. For me it's the deciding factor in turning a house into a home.

My personal style and design philosophy are reflective of my life and are richly layered with adventures—between my different lives on two continents, my friends, family, children and animals. All these things add so much of the color that goes into my work. Life should be lived fearlessly on a daily basis, and as with decorating a home, our lives are richer if we are willing to try things that include color.

This book illustrates what I've learned over the years and is a way to share some of the knowledge that I have accumulated during my lifelong love affair with materials. *Classic Country* is a reference tool for anyone who loves color, texture and layering of fabrics to help bring life to a room.

THE KITCHEN IS where I feel most comfortable. In my house this is where it all happens; it is the center and heart of the house. The kitchen is where my boys have learned to be creative and feel most at home.

I love to make people happy, and that generally means giving them food. Growing up, we lived in a flat overlooking one of London's great parks. My parents were "drawing room people." As was the custom of the day, my father was a real gentleman and my mother had grown up in Egypt having servants. They both treated the kitchen as a workplace and never as a social gathering point. But in my

KITCHENS
The Heart and Soul

heart, I always identified with the middle-class countryside life. Those wonderful homes outside the city felt alive, with people and dogs and family constantly coming and going, the kitchen cheerily filling up with house guests and lively conversation. I knew that once I had a home of my own, that's where I would be. And to this day, if you come into my home at any given moment, you're likely to find any of the three boys and me sitting around the center island, living our lives.

Cooking for two throws me, but not for twenty: two means soufflés; twenty means you're lucky if you get anything. With my houses in both Santa Monica and the south of France, I am constantly entertaining and cooking for a flow of friends and family.

When it came to remodeling my Santa Monica kitchen, I didn't have the luxury of great space when I knocked into the dining and living rooms. Instead of creating one big space, I continued the arch theme that is throughout the house and put in double pocket doors leading to the dining room, giving it the possibility of being separate but

There's something so down-to-earth about sitting in the kitchen. I'm always honored when someone shows me into their kitchen for a meeting. It's the soul of the home—the one room where there is no pretense. If a good chopping board and knife are all you can afford, then that's more than enough. Even when I have an office nearby, I end up working on my laptop on the kitchen island. It's comfortable, and I feel connected to the rest of the household; I like to be where the action is.

I'm so over upper cabinets; they make a room seem smaller and allow one to hoard.

also accomplishing the one-room feeling. The Spanish-style house was built in the early 1920s and reminds me of a farmhouse in southern Spain. I kept the kitchen's footprint. In the new room, two things dominate: a Damien Hirst picture and an Aga stove. An Aga makes all other cooking gadgets superfluous.

When I bought the house, there was barely enough money to pay the movers, so I did the minimum to make the place livable. Later, with the remodel, I had everything I wanted: cabinet shelves that glide in and out, a pantry where there is enough room to store everything, and an Aga.

The way we live nowadays, where space is so expensive, I would sacrifice a formal dining room and living room for a larger kitchen. When designing for either a client or myself, the kitchen always takes the most time, thought and energy. Knowing how to live simply has influenced the choices I make in my design work. Many times an idea evolves during the design process and the room takes a turn and ends up being different from what was expected at the outset. That's just part of the process and I believe you should go with your gut. Ideally you want a client not to be so rigid that ideas can't change. Being self-taught, I've had the luxury of changing things.

The mixture of different periods—with the Lloyd Loom chairs, Bauer pottery, an Aga and
Design Within Reach barstools—gives the room a timeless feel.

I always wanted to live in a barn. The informality of barn living is so appealing to me. *Pretense* and *importance* are two words I don't identify with.

FACING: This great room was once home to the blond Aquitaines, who were previous inhabitants. This former cow barn is now the soul of the house. We eat and live in community style in this room. The former manger is now used for displaying favorite dishes and doubles as a sideboard.

ABOVE: A simple table at work-top height is my most valued piece in the kitchen. I have only things that I use on a daily basis. Aesthetics are important but practicality a must.

BELOW: There's nothing to beat open-air markets, especially in France—the laughter, sense of style and riot of pure color everywhere you turn. It never fails to inspire my fabric designs. As the seasons change, so do the colors—from strawberry red to raspberry pink to eggplant aubergine. To me, all inspiration comes from day-to-day living. (Tarn et Garonne, France)

A rchitecture is but a frame for life, and a house becomes a home only with the warmth and colors of textiles, furnishings and, of course, people.

—Marc Appleton

LEFT: The manger was used to incorporate a fireplace into this large space. The fireplace skirt is indigenous to this part of France. Though lovely, it is not purely decorative; it protects from excess smoke when the fireplace fails to draw. Summer sofas are slipcovered in Kathryn Ireland green "Ticking."

BELOW: My new clients—just kidding. These were the previous occupants of the kitchen in southwest France.

A GREAT PAINTING

A harmonious

OR PHOTOGRAPH

mixture of old and new

ON THE WALL

living gives the room

MAKES THE KITCHEN

a timeless feel.

IMPORTANT.

After having spent a few summers at my home in France, the Oscar-winning actress Louise Fletcher came to stay and found a farmhouse a bike ride away. The house, like so many in the French countryside, was a complete ruin in the middle of a barren field, without even a dirt path leading to it. (Monclar du Quercy, France)

Louise took inspiration from my house, turning the cow barn into a kitchen, keeping the history of the house intact and renovating it to twenty-first-century standards. She lived at my house during the renovation process and managed the renovation herself, at the same time scouring the countryside for furnishings. Her study is an example of her eclectic good taste. The paintings scattered throughout the room are from her private collection and the fabrics throughout the house, needless to say, came from me.

BELOW: The farmer was taking no negotiation nonsense from me.

FOR THIS LONG ISLAND

kitchen, one of the focal points of the room is the antique light fixture, found locally at House of Christie's in Sag Harbor. For these clients I recolored my first fabric design, "Quilt," in butterscotch. These particular colors were inspired from the cathedral in Montauban (above). All of my color ideas come from local surroundings and everyday living, be it architecture, open-air markets or just the mud under my feet. I photograph anything that appeals to me and keep pictures haphazardly filed in various baskets in my closet and office. The baskets contain such random things as shells brought back from Bali, earth from the banks of the Nile and stones from Puglia.

This casual Connecticut kitchen has features that are very French country: well-used wooden countertops, a long farmhouse table, no above-counter cupboards and open shelving covered simply with linen towels.

We don't usually think of the kitchen as a place to display artwork and collections. But what a lively wall display the everyday plates make, set off by a black case. And the dog paintings? I can't think of anyplace where man's best friend isn't perfectly at home.

In my Connecticut kitchen I used Kathryn's red "Paisley" fabric, which made the room, strangely enough, both playful and majestic.

—Anne McNally

For Anne McNally's Connecticut farmhouse, the stage was already set. I just came in and helped her with fabric choices. This red paisley print was the first pattern I created and was such a success that I thought, wow—what has taken me so long to enter the textile business.

However, my confidence was a bit premature, as piles and piles of strike-offs that never worked soon made me feel that maybe the red paisley was just beginner's luck.

Once I got down the recipes and colors for each design and found the right ground cloth to print on, I was off to the races. The ground cloth is one of the most important elements in textile design. All fabrics take colors differently and it was only after having experimented on many different fibers that I decided to print on hemp.

☒ Plan the size of the island based on the activities you'll want to do there. Eat? Study? Craft? Make candy and bread? Gather your friends to help make the stew? The bigger the activities, the bigger the counter space needs to be.

☒ Avoid too many over-counter cabinets, as they are passé and make a room seem smaller.

☒ Utilize freestanding furniture rather than built-ins, and have some pieces custom made.

☒ Custom make built-ins to look like freestanding furniture.

IDEAS FOR THE PERFECT KITCHEN

☒ Give an old piece of furniture a new use. An antique dresser not only adds character to a room but also is just as practical as a cupboard for storing dishes and linens.

☒ A fireplace is a huge asset in the kitchen, especially if you fit it out with a cooking arm for using a dutch oven or build in a cove for baking bread and pizza.

☒ Good lighting on dimmers helps to easily transform your kitchen from a place for cooking to a space for entertaining.

SUNDAY LUNCH WHILE growing up was a formal affair—roast lamb, beef or pork with Yorkshire pudding, bread, sauce, the works—and always held in the dining room. Now, with my boys and me, Sunday lunch is held either on the beach or around the pool, in the kitchen or Dutch barn when in France, but rarely in the dining room. People don't live as formally as they used to, so the dining room is becoming a less-popular choice when designing a home. And often it multiplies into several uses, dining-cum-library-cum-workspace being the most common.

DINING AND BREAKFAST ROOMS

Space is so often an issue and you can easily incorporate a dining area in your kitchen. Less-formal spaces like the breakfast room are more and more likely to be used formally for dining also.

However, if you have the space and the means, then having a formal space for eating and entertaining is a nice luxury. A dining room is great for special occasions when you want to seat six to twelve people, or when having cozy get-togethers with family and friends. And there's no question it can be a center of activity if eating meals together is part of your family life.

Having a crowd over for an impromptu

party is much easier than a prearranged dinner for two or four, where a perfect meal might be expected along with 100 percent of my time! To me, a dining room is more for nighttime than for daytime use. My daytime parties are almost always outdoors, but I might be atypical in that I live in warm climates.

Growing up as children, we had to sit through long, boring meals with the grown-ups. I used the time to take in my surroundings. Some of my friends lived in extremely grand houses where we were served by butlers, and others, like our family, in a fisherman's cottage where we had to help ourselves.

I'm known for my parties. My mother was a great hostess and good at mixing people. It's really such an art but something that comes naturally to me. My most successful parties are the ones where the least amount of thought has gone into them. I've pulled together an eclectic crowd just from people I've seen that day.

Curtains are a must for nighttime dining. When closed at night with the room accented by candlelight, any decorating flaws are well masked. Candlelight is the star of any evening.

The home is our personal space. It reflects the character and uniqueness of the people who live there, not only the uniqueness of each individual, but how they combine with one another to form a cohesive unit. With architecture, color, furniture, fabrics, art and accessories we strive to create a feeling in the home that reflects our mutual desires.

—Leif

Working on the East Coast was always a challenge when my boys were small. Those little voices asking "How much longer, Mummy? When are you coming home?" were always difficult to hear. However, my times in Amagansett were made particularly fun by my friend Kari Lyn Sabin-Jones, who was so accommodating and became a great assistant. Between working with her and the architect Francis Fleetwood, I couldn't have had a better team. The eighteenth-century farmhouse project started out as a simple addition, but with its age, the engineers found it unsafe; in fact, the morning Kari Lyn was moving out for the remodel, she nearly fell through the dining room ceiling. The house ended up being torn down and rebuilt, much to the Sabins' dismay. However, Francis managed effortlessly to re-create the feel of the original house by duplicating many of its original features.

Playing with Tradition

Hand-dyed linens for curtains, mixed with Indian embroideries
and Turkish cloths, adds a contemporary freshness
that stops a room from looking old-fashioned.

—Victoria Tenant

If I remember correctly, the point of reference in this dining room came from the painting of fruit. The burnt sienna color used on the walls and curtains made the room extremely cozy while still providing an air of elegance. The custom-made chairs were copied from Italian originals, the only difference being that these are much more comfortable. The seat depth is wide, and the additional padding on the backs makes for a comfortable long evening.

A WELL-CHOSEN

Sprinkle sun-washed spaces

FABRIC CAN CREATE

with the right combination of the

A CALMING

unexpected anchored by a

TRANSITION FROM

sense of flow and color.

ROOM TO ROOM.

Kathryn Ireland has always made

me want to find my dream house so I can start from scratch and cover everything in all of her fabrics! They evoke cosy European houses where life has been lived happily in the garden or in front of the fire.

—Wendy Goodman

For a dining room north of the Spanish border, color was not key. More important was the juxtaposition of the objects in the room: a French table and chairs from the 1940s, seventeenth-century German prints, eighteenth-century candlesticks, contemporary zebra-print rug. All of these objects now live together harmoniously in a house dating back to the sixteenth century. A casual blend of rusticity and elegance, this room is ready for an intimate dinner party or lighthearted family dining, whichever the day requires.

For my friend Leslie in Brentwood, California, the use of beige in her dining room was not an option. She had a preexisting striped valance that she had found at a flea market and wanted to keep in the room, but otherwise I had free reign. By mixing bright colors, different fabric patterns and checkerboard painted floors, the room feels a far cry from suburban Los Angeles.

On a trip to Guatemala (a blind date, in fact), I came across these ladies carrying fabulous pots with a strie effect on them. This was the inspiration for my "Ikat Stripe" fabric.

A successful room is

one that doesn't try too hard, is physically and visually

comfortable and manages to delight the people living there over time.

—Jackie Terrell

Some antique plates from Limoges found at the Albi flea market were the finishing touch to decorating this breakfast room. The antiqued green Lloyd Loom chairs, found locally in Country Gear in Bridgehampton, have become one of my decorating staples.

If you can gather together all or part of these dining room features, you'll be well prepared for hosting with a lot of confidence and a minimum of trouble:

🖎 A great chandelier.

🖎 Good lighting—candles whenever possible.

🖎 An expandable table.

🖎 A variety of great table linens, including some colorful ones and white Irish linens for more formal occasions.

🖎 Comfortable chairs for long nights at the table.

🖎 Simple silver—I found a complete Deco set at a local flea market in France. It's also fun to start collecting a simple design from Christofle; as you scout antiques markets, you can pick up a few pieces here and there and also add to it from the store.

FAVORITE DINING ROOM FEATURES

🖎 White plates are my favorite; they make a good backdrop for food.

🖎 Glasses—I like to mix and match colors and sizes, which makes collecting easy and fun!

🖎 Reds and earth tones are my favorites for the dining room. Warmer tones are better for rooms used mostly in the evenings with low-level lighting.

🖎 Arrange the space to double as a library, workplace, or maybe even a guest room.

🖎 With space so limited, books lend themselves well to the dining room.

THE LIVING ROOM, once a formal place commonly known as the drawing room in England, was where the ladies retired to gossip after dinner while the men sat in the dining room and smoked cigars and drank port. Times have changed. The stiffness of an older generation has given way to a relaxed elegance that suits the way we live now. Clients who come to me are not looking for a re-creation of a bygone era; they are looking for an interpretation for today's lifestyle. They want to live well, but as relaxed as possible in a hectic world.

LIVING ROOMS
Family Rooms, Morning Rooms and Studies

I grew up in a house full of memories, and until I was ten or so, I thought that antiques were things that one simply had. I had no idea that you could buy them some-where. Though my childhood living room was quite full of objects—Japanese lacquer tables, baubles, curios, a grand piano and treasures from any number of exotic trips that family members had taken—it still felt very personal.

My own house is an eclectic mix of old and new, modern and traditional, antiques and reproductions.

Color is always my starting point. My own houses have evolved over the years, and while the seat covers may have changed, the warmth and feel of the rooms have remained the same.

Individual style is how you put things together. A room should tell your story, remind you of where you've been, who you've known. I used to think that having a decorator was a very impersonal thing, but what a good decorator does is translate the ideas of the client into a well-produced format. Some clients are at first unable to describe what they want, so the decorator's job is to extract images from their minds and turn them into rooms. Not an easy job. It isn't just getting the size of the lamp shade right or the puddle of the curtain exact. It means being an editor, a life enhancer and, ultimately, a friend.

I remember exactly where, when and with whom I bought all the things in my house; e.g., the Moroccan pot on the coffee table was hand-carried back from a trip only to be smashed to pieces when some fellow traveler threw his backpack on top of it.

As a decorator color becomes my energy. . . . It feeds my mind and in turn my creativity. But fabric is my true passion, the texture, touch, even the weave makes me smile from the inside out. Kathryn knows the perfect recipe for this cocktail and combines both in such symmetry that the taste is so delicious it leaves you wanting more . . . Much, much more!

—Martyn Laurence Bullard

Fabric is my starting point

when I think about a room—curtain fabric, then sofas and chairs. A room without fabric is like a party without drink: flat and joyless and never quite takes off. In fact, I generally find that a strong fabric is the most memorable feature of a room. I remember the curtain material when the pictures, furniture, paint and even the guests are long forgotten. Kathryn Ireland's fabrics are not only exquisite, they are also so useable. They are like Kathryn herself; they travel well and you can take them anywhere, and they will always amuse and put you in a good mood.

—Nicholas Coleridge

BELOW: Nicholas Coleridge was my first client. While studying in London for my A levels, one of which was Textile and Design, there was a certain amount of practice that had to be done. Nick had just moved into his first flat, a basement in Chelsea, and hired me to make him pillows. It was only at the dinner given at San Lorenzo in London when launching my fabric line in 1997 that he asked me why they cost so much: he could have bought them off the shelf a lot cheaper. I remembered that the deal was hourly and I had rather cheekily included unpicking and restitching time!

In this sunroom in Brentwood, California, the light can be so intense during the morning hours that curtains are a must. Combining soft florals and stripes in linens was my way of making this a real morning room—a place to read the paper, answer letters and entertain friends.

Kathryn Ireland

ROBERT KIME

SINCE MOVING TO

California in my early twenties, going home has always been critical for my well-being and keeping sight of my past. Any excuse to go back to London and I'm there. When I began designing textiles, I opened a showroom in London for that very reason. But any reason will prolong my stay, even if it's simply to upholster my host's flat. James Holland Hibbert has an art gallery in St. James specializing in modern British art. When I need to find art for clients, James and his partner, Hugo de Ferranti, are my first and only call. Even though their speciality is modern, Hazlitt Holland Hibbert, the parent company, deals in all periods. Visiting Berry Street is like going on a private tour of an art gallery. Spread over four floors and across two buildings, a morning there with the boys is the equivalent of a week's lecture at the Tate.

James's flat overlooks the Chelsea embankment. His only criteria was that the fabrics not overshadow the art (he had chosen the wrong house guest for an opinion on the matter). He wanted instant gratification, so we whizzed off to Robert Kime's shop in Kensington Church Street and bought up his stock of exquisitely embroidered pillows.

clarence house
www.clarencehouse.com
email: info@clarencehouse.com
2 Henry Adams Street, San Francisco, CA 94103, 415-431-0100

2 yard minimum
Memo samples are due in 30 days
Samples not returned or damaged will be billed to your account

W hen I enter a room I tend to look at the fabrics used in it in the same way that I look at the books in a person's library. I become judgmental and biased, and tend to judge the room's owners by their choice of materials. It is not the right attitude, and yet fabrics create that reaction in me. I either love them or hate them, but they never leave me cold.

—Miguel Flores Vianna

Like me, my client and friend Nancy has three boys. This is a dark room that we wanted to make as cozy and comfortable as possible. Over the years, I've helped in almost every room of the house. As it was with the rest, Nancy basically decorated it herself; my job was to assist with the fabric and color. This room is a great example of Nancy's wonderful eye for detail and decorating; the collection of porcelain, pottery and china is very personal, and it was from these objects that I found inspiration for the color scheme used in the rest of the house.

Julia Louis-Dreyfus and Brad Hall's home on the beach in Santa Barbara is one house I'd like to live in myself. They originally purchased the home as a summertime beach residence, which they renovated so successfully that it became a semi-permanent home for the Hollywood couple and their two children. The house, which sits right on the sea, was designed by the great eco-friendly architect David Hertz. He created a modern home that has all the attributes to make this the perfect weekend retreat. Julia was lovely to have insisted that my fabrics be used throughout the home to create a soft, beachy feel to the rooms. I used fabrics from my Balinese-inspired collection in rich browns and blues—a chic combination. Julia and Brad were dream clients, always excited and enthusiastic—important adjectives in this business.

Kathryn Ireland: What does fabric mean to you?

David Mamet: Fabric means to me that which keeps me from sitting on the springs.

Walking into the Mamets' living room for the first time brought a smile to my face. My fabric on the pillows and a chair were staring me in the face. When David and Rebecca moved from the East Coast to Santa Monica, they asked for my help in renovating the kitchen and bathrooms. Their style, like mine, is informal but elegant. I love helping to create homes, not showcases.

It's fabulous to have my fabrics side by side with Kathryn's. They complement each other in unexpected ways.

—Nina Campbell

Over the years of summers in France, I've spent endless days biking and driving down lanes that led to dilapidated houses in search of homes for friends. Louise Fletcher was the first to decamp from my house and become my neighbor. Anne McNally and I even got as far as meeting neighboring farmers with checkbook in hand when she looked across the valley at my house in the distance and said in her very French accent, "Why do I want a house here when I want to be over there with all of you?" She had a point, so we decided we would just pool our homes and we would all be welcome at each other's homes. All of a sudden, I had homes in Paris, New York and Connecticut.

Color ideas come from everyday living and what inspires me that day.

The striped fabric in Kate and Ben Goldsmith's London study is from my pumpkin phase.

Having started my textile career hand-printing, which was enough of a challenge, it wasn't until a few years later that I started to weave. It seemed crazy not to offer coordinates to go with the prints. The idea of designers searching design centers for wovens to go with my "not run of the mill" (no pun intended) color sense seemed a shame.

It was off to Como to find a weaver. Like going to any trade show, I was bombarded by so much to look at, but it was very apparent to me which were the best mills. With my knowledge of which way the warp and weft ran, I added a section of wovens to the line that now account for nearly half the collection.

A PATCHWORK OF

Versatility is key when

COLOR AND

blending patterns and designs~

TEXTURE IS

giving personality to a room

ACCENTUATED BY

without overwhelming.

NATURAL LIGHT.

There were only two things I asked Kathryn for when she redesigned my apartment: one was to have hardwood floors in case I feel like dancing and the second was a table by my bed for my martini.

—Leah Adler

A busy working woman who runs her own successful Beverly Hills restaurant, Leah Adler and I were thrown together when her son and daughter-in-law, Steven and

Kate Spielberg, asked me to help redecorate her apartment. I was delighted to help old family friends but had no idea how much fun Leah and I would have together. Her love of life

was so inspirational, and the fact that she gave me control over what stayed and went is a tribute to the extraordinary lady she is. The look of joy on Leah's face when she walked in

the door for the first time six weeks later was compensation for all the heartache and bad moments I have had with other clients over the years.

Relaxed, comfortable living is how

most of us envision life in the country. The pretension of the city is left behind and one can lie back and enjoy the change of pace that country life brings. Many of the interiors in this book are set in urban surroundings. Even more so when living in cities, we want to come home to simple elegance and timeless interiors.

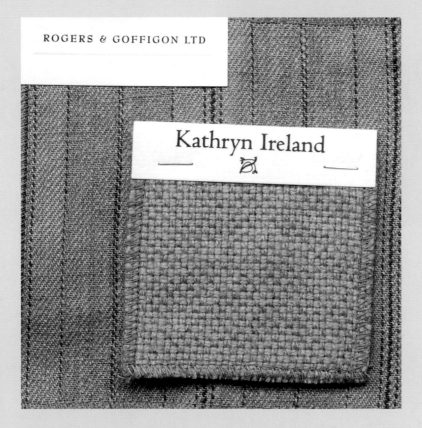

ROGERS & GOFFIGON LTD

Kathryn Ireland

The fun part of being a decorator is giving new life to old things. Everyone has hand-me-downs and pieces that can't be sent to the Salvation Army for fear that an aging aunt should ask where her wedding present is. Sometimes it's just a simple slipcover or a new lamp shade and other times it's a distressed coat of paint. All it sometimes takes is a keen, fresh eye to glance over one's belongings and spot the treasures worth saving.

FACING: For this Brentwood, California, house we transformed the master bedroom into an upstairs sitting room when an addition was built on. By using muted colors and luxurious textures for the fabrics, the artwork is permitted to take center stage.

This house was torn down and rebuilt after finding major structural damage. It was an eighteenth-century wooden farmhouse, and my clients really wanted to respect what had been there before. Paying close attention to period details so the original feel of the home was re-created, the most important piece we found was the beautiful hand-carved Queen Anne mantelpiece bought from House of Christie's in Sag Harbor. The painting and candleholders are also late-eighteenth century.

One the great lessons of this home is the idea that buying one or two important pieces can make a room. The room is a mixture of pieces new to the family as well as some that hold some personal value to the clients. The extraordinary part of this achievement that Francis Fleetwood created was a house that had immediate age and character.

W̲hen you walk into a house designed by Kathryn, you automatically assume the owner has impeccable taste.

—Gene Washington

Kathryn Ireland's success stems from her own personal style. Her approach is one of refined simplicity. Practical taste along with a balance of color and pattern are her trademarks.

—John Rosselli

This was a daring room not only for my client but also for me. I obviously knew that if the walls turned out to be too overpowering I could always repaint them—it wouldn't be the end of the world. But it couldn't have turned into a cozier room.

OVER

the years, some high-profile decorators have been involved with this picturesque Queen Anne house overlooking Richmond Park—most notably John Fowler and Nina Campbell. So I was honored that Annabel, who I have known all my life, allowed me to give my input. She wanted to transform this one-time bedroom into a cozy upstairs living room where she could watch television with her many grandchildren and relax with her dogs.

The beautiful proportions of this room coupled with the wonderful light made for an inspirational project. Using a mixture of old documents, Robert Kime, Colfax and Fowler, and my fabrics, the room has been imbued with a lived-in feel. The curtains are hung from McKinney and Company hand-carved curtain poles. Shona, an old school friend, known as the Queen of Knobs, makes exquisite hand-crafted poles and finials.

For me, some of the most magical

environments in the world have been given their special atmosphere through the use of fabric. I think of Mongiardino's dining room for Lee Radziwill—a room lined with wonderfully old-fashioned Romany gypsy scarves, glazed and overpainted by Lila de Nobilis—such a simple device that created a room out of Turgenev. Or the simple sprigged Indian cottons he used to create a sense of immense seraglio luxury at the Brandolini's palazzo in Venice. And then there is the Napoleonic ticking stripe tented room at Malmaison....

—Hamish Bowles

Layering of patterns terrifies most people, but there are times when you have to take a chance and do something daring.

My old friend Catherine Hesketh has confidently thrown together a variety of patterns and colors with aplomb. The success of the room is that one object, color, or design is not more important than another.

At the end of it all,

fabric sets the character of a room. By the choice of fabric the mood of a room transforms from a simple calm summer's day with rumpled white linens and cool sexy voiles to a cozily cluttered eclectic haven with red paisleys and warm velvets to snuggle up to.

—Rachel Ashwell

The use of color and how it's assembled in a room creates the picture, but there is no school that teaches the eye color. While nearly everybody has some feelings about color, not everyone has good instincts about combining and layering colors.

To overthink or over-produce a room is a major mistake. Unless you have gut instincts about mixing fabrics and blending textures and patterns, it's better to rely on a decorator's sense. I love it when clients trust my gut instincts. They're always surprised and delighted with the results.

I think it was partly due to my parents' antiques collections that I have wanted to create for myself and clients the "instant memories" feeling that a room full of great things has to offer. Here's how to do it:

🖉 Choose a grounding antique for the room—a piece that is big enough to have presence but not so large as to overwhelm the rest of your furnishings. If you don't have a family heirloom, there's nothing wrong with purchasing one; a sideboard, an armoire or a table that carries another family's history is still a legitimate focal point for your living room.

🖉 Blend bright with muted colors in an orchestration of design and pattern that truly reflects who you are and how you live. The living room should revolve around your favorite colors. Red is my favorite color for the living room because it brings

ELEMENTS OF A SUCCESSFUL LIVING ROOM

life and happiness to the room where family gathers and friends are welcome. For me this color heightens the senses and even stimulates conversations.

🖉 Mix high with low to create drama: a tall armoire with a low coffee table; large mirrors with small oil paintings; high ceilings with low-hung lighting. Proportion is always key in decorating,

🖉 Combine heirlooms with new furnishings for interesting contrasts. Pillows, lamps and club fenders in modern fabrics, colors and textures are easy companions for many periods and styles of antique furnishings.

🖉 Use unexpected details. On my fireplace I sunk three tiles depicting a flying lady into the plaster—very Pre-Raphaelite and adds color to the off-white plaster.

🖉 Steer away from having a television in the formal room. Even with flat screens becoming more attractive, one should still have a specific out-of-the-way space where you can tuck up and watch a program.

THE WELL-TRAVELED areas that take you from one room to the next are just as important as any other space. So whether you have a large entry to your home or a tiny one, these transitional spaces shouldn't be neglected. A very simple entryway needs only a shaker peg, a hat rack or a trunk to give it some sense of being and purpose. These minimal furnishings can bring a small entry to life.

With space limitations, you can't treat these spaces as you would a room. I look at transitional spaces like art galleries: they should take you from one room to the next and lead you there both physically and visually.

Landings, for instance, are often not large enough for much of anything. Placing a narrow bookcase or a window treat-

ENTRY WAYS
Hallways, Mudrooms, Landings

ment—should you have a window to work with—is a great way to give the architecture purpose. For example, a client's house in Brentwood had a good-sized landing, so we set up a place to sit, making it cozy and comfortable by putting in a Chesterfield leather chair and creating a masculine, studylike library in this area that would have otherwise gone unused.

Though I say that the living room is the first space you see upon entering my home in Santa Monica, the mudroom (it's hardly a room) is really what you encounter first. Here you'll always see my three sons' sports equipment, muddied shoes and book bags. Though it may not always look perfectly tidy, this space signals to anyone who enters that mine is a casual home that never takes itself too seriously.

My hallway in southern France has a simple haberdasher's table to one side with a pair of Vaughan tea caddy lamps. Terra-cotta tiles to match the original were found locally.

The collection of Jesuit priest prints

found in the English countryside, once framed, fit perfectly into what would otherwise have been a difficult area to find artwork for. It turned out that these unimportant-looking prints were original eighteenth-century copperplate engravings.

So always be on the lookout and never pass by that little shop that you'd just love to pop into if only there were time. You never know! Where I live in France, between Montauban and Albi—homes to two of France's greatest artists: Toulouse Lautrec and Ingres—I'm always hoping that I'll stumble across an original at one of the many summer flea markets.

The rough-hewn, hand-embroidered Indian textile draped over the center table was something I brought back from an adventure in Delhi with my great friends Abu Janie and Sandeep Kosler, who I met doing a reality TV show in England a few years back. The color combinations have inspired fabrics in my collection.

Overly decorated houses always

strike me as feeling vaguely impersonal. To me a real home always has small fragments of bad taste mixed in amongst beautiful fabrics and furniture; a scribbled drawing done by a child propped up next to a work of art, a quirky ashtray stolen to commemorate a delicious lunch, a souvenir from a flea market. These are the things that make a house look lived in. Kathryn's genius is in instantly creating a past through her use of colors, textures and muted fabrics. Her houses feel like home.

—Sarah Standing

A splash of red in the right

place makes all the difference to the energy of the room.

FACING: When restoring a house, the biggest challenge is restraint—not redoing everything. In the pigeoniere, I kept the great old stone floors. Cracked they may be, but all of those years of history enhance the beauty of the place. One house guest managed to frighten the boys by insisting that people were trying to come up through the floor stone.

The stable door, old pine desk, bread oven paddle and loose-fitting cream slipcovers make this both an entryway and a living space. My neighbor Mary's photographs cover the walls; owning a Monet or Renoir doesn't interest me unless I have discovered it myself. I much prefer hanging family and friends' photos, children's artwork or pieces I've picked up on my travels.

ABOVE: The silk shade and turned-wood candlestick make a classy lamp.

WHEN

planning an entryway, one of the pieces I always try to find space for is a bench upon which coats may be tossed and shoes may be tied. There is something very welcoming about having a place to sit down on as soon as you enter the house. A certain amount of clutter is expected, but having storage in these areas—a bench with under-seat storage or a cupboard with or without doors—is key to controlling it.

ENTRYWAYS

Articles of clothing

SHOULD BE

and neatly arranged

PRACTICAL AND

personal objects can turn

ALSO PLEASING TO

into artwork if aesthetically placed.

LOOK AT.

This upstairs landing in Brentwood was the perfect place to turn into a sitting area. Mixing a leather chesterfield with a pair of French chairs, Tibetan horn lamp from Pat McGann and my client's existing furniture transforms this otherwise wasted space into additional seating for a house full of men. Proportion in furniture is key. Although there are multiple patterns used in this space, the overall look is still soothing to the eye. Decorating is like cooking: one too many ingredients and the flavor is ruined; too few and there is no taste at all.

The marble table in a New York

town house entry hall was purchased in the depths of the English countryside and then shipped to New York before realizing it wouldn't fit through the front door. It is such a heavy table, and unfortunately we had to hoist it in through a window!

Taking the window out first, of course. I think between the shipping and the installation, the table was almost a "give-away." But it makes a dramatic statement and sets the tone for the rest of this grand urban home.

The client told me she wanted her New York home to have the feel of my French guesthouse, the Pigeoniere. It was cream, but cream taken to the next level—Chelsea textile crewel work instead of your basic duck cotton.

Transitional spaces— hallways, mudrooms and landings— are often the perfect places for injections of color and life. Putting artwork on the walls, especially pieces created by family members, adds personality to spaces that often don't have personalization. I love to reframe clients' old photos in different-sized frames to create an album that can be looked at every day.

Hallways and staircases are great for a little bit of humor or for stenciling a pattern on the walls.

In many French homes, the entry hallway takes you straight to another room or right out to a garden; these pass-through rooms are often generous, wide spaces. There is enough room in my hallway that I can display a collection of local pots and still have room for a bench and a piano. I

CREATIVE IDEAS FOR ENTRYWAYS, HALLWAYS, MUDROOMS AND LANDINGS

always say a house should have a piano even if you don't play it. Someone inevitably will know how.

Never hide who you are. What your house looks like is not as important as how you live in it—as long as the mess is well organized and there's a reason for it being there.

A chest or cupboard will help control clutter.

Floor furniture should provide a resting or changing place without getting in the way of traffic flow.

Use baskets for everything from umbrellas to muddy boots; they work fantastically.

THE BEDROOM IS a favorite room of mine. It's a place to entertain, work and sleep. Although an intimate space, I like to invite friends up for a quick chat or perhaps to share some news or just lie together watching the television. I've even screened my friend's movie from here.

Less is always more is my mantra for perfect living. Good linens, interesting books by the bed, fresh-cut flowers. Something I don't advocate: a TV in the bedroom. But there is nothing not to like about snuggling up in bed with a fab film.

BEDROOMS
MASTER, GUEST AND KIDS'

When positioning your bedroom in the home, allow for morning light to stream through the windows. (Unless you work nights, blackout fabric is so nineties.) I can always tell what time it is in the early morning by the light that comes through the curtains and sheers. That's part of being in tune with the world. In the eco-friendly environment that we have to live in today, houses must become more practical and less decorative.

My friend, interior designer George Terbovitch was always there to steer me in the right direction when I was getting started in the business. He is the master of practical jokes, and when he insisted I used Raoul's "Chinari" in red for the interior bed curtain fabric, I wasn't sure at first if he was kidding. This was before my own fabric line had been born.

The extravagance of K's personality is reflected in the her creativity. Her work successfully mixes her British traditions with her Californian experiences.

—George Terbovich

Constantly experimenting and renovating my homes—my personal internship—I learned so much so quickly. This red fabric was the stimulus for designing my first collection. It was April and I drove to Santa Barbara to meet Sally McQuillan at the Raoul Factory. I said I thought I had a fabric collection in me and would she be interested in printing it for me. It was love at first sight. Our kids have grown up together listening to us discuss heat settings, colorways and screen techniques. Sally showed me the way.

We grew up like gypsies,
sleeping in one big bed.

—Otis Weis

Being a Leo, regal is an adjective I identify
with.Bed curtains give a majestic air to
any bedroom.

My bedroom in Santa Monica has a
wonderful high-pitched ceiling that is perfect for a four-poster bed. Atypical of the
Spanish houses in the area, which have
smaller rooms, if any, on the first floor,
this house was added on to in the seven-
ties, and matching the height of the living
room ceiling was a priority.

Having a mirror or painting over the
bed in earthquake-prone southern
California is not sensible, so what to do
with all that space? For me, it's the perfect opportunity to dress the bed, giving a
sense of grandeur to the room. Climbing
into bed with my laptop and books, with
boys the other side of the hallway, is all I
look forward to at the end of a long day.

My guest bedroom was rather spooky owing to the old legend of the murder that took place there in the eighteenth century. Then Kathryn came to the rescue and transformed it by using her vibrant colors into one of the prettiest and coziest rooms in the house.

—Lady Annabel Goldsmith

By that September I was ready to take the first collection to Decorex, the annual trade show for interior design in London. It was by chance that someone had fallen out at the last minute, making way for my stand. The show was held in Richmond, a small town on the edge of the Thames. Lady Annabel Goldsmith, who has been in my life for as long as I can remember, let me experiment with my new collection on one of her guest bedrooms. I upholstered the walls in yellow tonal ticking, dressed the bed and made window treatments in red paisley stripe, and covered the bench at the foot of the bed in green paisley. These were three of my first designs. The remaining designs I incorporated into a patchwork quilt for the bed. And now i have a room of my own to sleep in whenever I stay in Surrey.

Patchwork quilts have become my

signature. Winning the needlework prize for my patchwork at the age of seven has stayed with me. It's also a great way to get rid of remnants. For one of my guest bedrooms in France, I found two similar armoires from a local French farmer, who was delighted to get the small amount of money I offered him.

I painted them both the same color and they looked like a very chic pair. This can be done with any two similar pieces of furniture; it's a simple way of tricking the eye into believing they are a pair. The chairs are covered in chenille bedcovers bought off the rack and then whipped into slipcovers. I have a feeling I made these myself!

CURTAINS ARE ONE

of the biggest investments in any room. When budget is a concern, I use a less-expensive plain fabric for the curtain yardage and dress it up with a wide band of printed fabric on the leading edge, bordered with the plain to pull the two fabrics together as a unit.

With Kathryn, you can
shut your eyes, open them five months later, and everything will be perfect.

—Steve Martin

BENNISON

THE FINE ARTS BUILDING
232 EAST 59TH STREET
NEW YORK NY 10022
TEL: 212.223.0373 FAX: 212.223.0655

The choice of fabrics in this Beverly Hills attic guest room was made in keeping with the country feel of the home. This one-time cottage was added on to using wood from the rafters of an old East Coast barn. A wool quilt, hand-painted lamps and a hooked rug make this simple room come alive.

EVEN THOUGH

the color scheme is feminine, the fabrics are rather offset by the masculinity of the furniture. For this guest room in Amagansett on Long Island, which is bathed in light from generous windows, we found some pieces locally in Bridgehampton to augment the existing bed and make the space more homey. Whenever a client has existing favorite pieces or family heirlooms, I try to let those pieces come forward in the room scheme. Rather than starting from scratch, I love giving new life to things that have sentimental value.

Everyone says my room is their favorite—it is very bright and pretty. I chose the colors when I was younger but I still really like it now.

—Kitty Halsey

Anne Halsey and I have worked together since the days of my little shop on Main Street that I had with Amanda Pais, where I turned some of my collection of antique textiles into pillows. When Anne bought a little hamlet in Gaillac, France, needless to say, I insisted on helping her with it.

A SUCCESSFUL

child's room is one where the child will be happy through their early years—nothing too infantile. When doing the bones of the room, take into consideration elements that might need to change through the many phases from baby to teenager. Window treatments especially are an investment, so use fabric that can make the transition. A new area rug and bedding are quick fixes for any child's or teenager's room. This one is in Amagansett, Long Island.

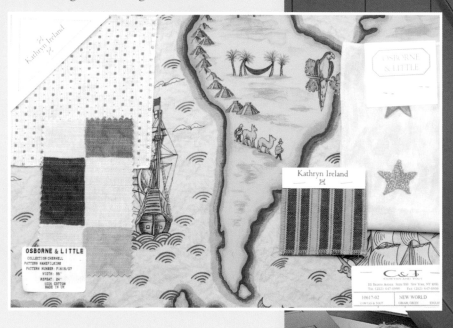

My room is like being on a safari, where
I feel like I can travel around the world
without ever leaving it.

—Sam Sabin

I love Kathryn's Gitana fabric in blue and green for the boys' bedrooms; it so beachy and serene.

—Julia Louis-Dreyfus

For the beach house my client and I decided to refinish Pottery Barn tables, beds and nightstands to be less white to perfectly match the cream in the Gitana fabric that was used in both green and blue colorway.

THE GUEST BEDROOM

should feel like you've walked into the perfect hotel room, except that you know by the books, carafe of water and fresh-cut flowers beside the bed that you have been welcomed into someone's home. If possible, the only difference from your own bedroom should be fewer personal touches such as photographs of loved ones and memorabilia. For the guest room in my Santa Monica home, I upholstered the walls to give it a sense of quiet. There is something very luxurious about using the same fabric on the walls and for the curtains. It gives a sense of continuity and in a small space makes the room cozy without being overwhelming.

K athryn's fabrics are a total reflection of her personality—vibrant, captivating, completely original, and classy. Every time I walk into my bedroom it's like she's there . . . only without all the talking!

—Tricia Brock

With so many windows in her New Preston, Connecticut, bedroom and in keeping with the Balinese bed, Anne wanted a clean look. Roman shades were the answer for the window treatments.

ABOVE: My black Arabs Twigs, Nazullah and Osiris grazing in their paddock in France. The intense, verdant hills of my farm inspired the green of my "Ikat" fabric.

BELOW: Having your clothes organized and being able to treat your closet as a room are heavenly. When building a house today, there is no excuse (except money) not to include a mudroom, laundry room and dressing room. They are the spine of modern living.

RECYCLING,

Both soothing and vibrant

SWAP MEETS AND

colors can make a room

SLEEPOVERS

peaceful and tranquil

ARE IN. EXCESS IS

without too much effort.

FINALLY OVER.

Kathryn Ireland's fabric, with its organic patterned inspirations of nature, work as a beautiful foil to an architecture of simplicity and natural materials.

—David Hertz

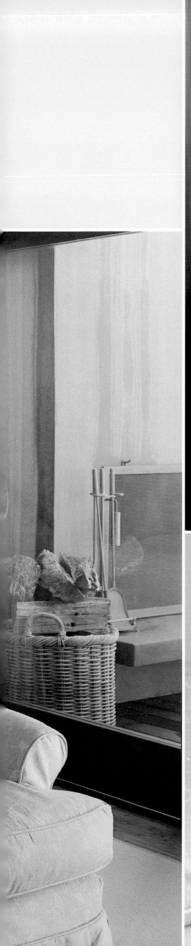

To counterbalance the simplicity and contemporary nature of the building in Montecito where Dreyfus and Hall have their home, Julia and I felt it a necessary to have some antiques. The Biedermeier chest was purchased from Leif Almont and paired with a Vaughan Declomana lamp.

There is nothing like the architecture of eighteenth-century
homes. These rooms are
timeless. The slanting floors
and irregular ceiling heights
illustrate how the places have
been added on to over the
years and how the foundations
have settled—charm that no
amount of money can buy.

Grandmother's bedroom
suite, which had long been in
storage, was resurrected in this
Gaillac, France, home. The
choice of yellow in this room
was inspired by the view of
sunflower fields seen out the
window. Curtain fabric is
Kathryn Ireland yellow "Ikat";
headboard, bed skirt and lamp
shade are "Small Check";.
chaise is yellow "Ribbed."

Mixing up two Fortuny prints in the same color-way with white sheers and adding a four-poster bed transforms this Brentwood, California, bedroom into the room I always envisioned for my clients. When reproducing antiques, they really must look like antiques, so the finish is key. If you are going for modern and clean, imperfections are not necessary.

The fabric is overwhelmingly feminine, while the dark furniture maintains a masculine feel.

All the fabrics make the room

relaxed and comfortable. The colors are soft and restful, and the curtain fabric has an irregular feel that makes it look blockprinted and contrasts with the check on the bed. I love the splashes of red.

—Ann Halsey

My favorite fabric combinations —stripe, check and pattern— are illustrated in this Gaillac bedroom. Local French antiques, reupholstered and refinished, are featured prominently.

Kathryn Ireland

The beauties of Louise's bedroom in Montclar de Quercy, France, which was originally the old kitchen, are the large working fireplace and the door to the outside. Louise's diverse mixture of Swedish-American and French antiques, plus her collection of nineteenth- and twentieth-century paintings, put her house in a class of its own. The different tones of blues in the furniture—from French gray to Swedish gray to more vibrant blues in both the lamps and the painting over the desk—are reflected in the color tones of the fabrics.

No matter what the season, this particular shade of Kathryn's blue linen I've chosen for my own bedroom (solid for the curtains and the same shade repeated in the patterns for cushions) gives me the peace and calm I need . It is one of the most beautiful colors I've ever used anywhere.

—Louise Fletcher

When planning a master bedroom for a married couple, the woman often wants something feminine and the man wants shades of blue and a masculine feel. Design is about finding a marriage of the two. The distressed wooden mantelpiece lends a bit of roughness,and the high-backed overstuffed chairs with clean lines strike a balance between femininity and masculinity. Punches of color on the bed pillows add another dimension to the subtle, soft blue tones used throughout the room in Amagansett, Long Island.

It's really fun because you get to sleep with more than three people, but you hit your head when you stand up, the ceilings are so low.

—Louis Weis

FACING: For three attic bedrooms in my Verlac, France, farmhouse, I used the floral design in three colorways—in this attic bedroom, the diamond batik fabric all the way: in Roman shades, slipper chair and bedcoverings

ABOVE: This room can sleep five kids; it's where all the fun takes place.

One summer my brother and I converted the attic. We plastered and sanded the floors ourselves. If you look closely at the photo you won't argue with me on that one. Plastering is one of those things that looks much easier than it is unless you are very experienced. I also added seagrass area rugs trimmed to match the room's color scheme. It is amazing what fabric can do to a room.

Although furniture and paintings immediately catch the eye, it is the color of the room, choice and texture of chosen fabric that ultimately set the mood. Just as a continued motif created with pale blue indicates a cool aura another made up with Sienna pink suggests warmth; both showing that colors in a home can never be underestimated.

—Natasha Fraser-Cavassoni

These attic bedrooms are simply furnished with recovered deck chairs and old wicker. Seagrass on the floor covers my bad sanding job.

FAR LEFT: Red floral fabric and an antique patchwork quilt dominate the room. A simple cupboard is curtained off in the corner of the room.

ABOVE: Kathryn Ireland "Tulip" pattern in pink is a window treatment and also covers my favorite bed from my teenage years.

BELOW: Another view of the same bedroom reveals a curtain door in "Tulip." I rescued an inexpensive deck chair whose outdoor days were over and recovered it in my pink "Ticking"; it makes a perfect catchall for clothes.

Once the architecture work

is done, decorating is all about the fabric. Fabric is the most flexible tool to achieve effect in a room. Fabrics supply us with color and pattern. They create a sense of comfort and, above all, atmosphere.

—Peter Dunham

The boys and I are frequent guests at the divine beach house of California-based interior designer Peter Dunham in Cadaquez, on the Costa Brava in Spain just north of Barcelona (below). There is no electricity and the outdoor bathroom was somewhat of a shock to my little LA boys. Here Peter uses my "Ikat Stripe" in firehouse red for his window treatments in West Hollywood.

IT WAS only when my LA showroom closed that I reconnected with my friend Windsor Smith. Our kids went to preschool together and she had been one of the early visitors to Verlac. She has been a supportive user of my fabrics over the years, so much so that she has even used some of my indigos in her own bedroom. Like me, Windsor turned her mothering skills to decorating.

"Every room for me begins with color. I usually prefer offbeat combinations of pattern and color when creating a storyboard. When I first met Kathryn, what struck me was what an amazing and colorful storyteller she was. It would only make sense that she would display that same mastery in her fabric designs. Kathryn's fabrics are all part of things wonderful. Classic, playful, smart and timeless prints derived from classic themes like the paisley, English floral, even Indian-inspired batiks and dhurrie resembling stripes interpreted in a way that is uniquely her own brand of English casual chic. They give every room a lived-in feeling and all seem to meld together perfectly in a way that appears that you picked them up all along the way. In my personal bedroom I created a canopy of her fabrics with layers of mismatched pillows in nearly all of her indigo patterns mixed in with vintage batiks and hand-dyed hemps. One of my favorite Sunday-afternoon hobbies is to rearrange them over and over again, because each combination is more beautiful than the one before."

—Windsor Smith

If a Tester four-poster bed is not in the cards, a simple oversized headboard makes a statement and fills up that space over the pillows.

A mosquito net with a cap on it is a quick and easy way to dress the bed.

It's so easy to find good-looking linens.

You don't need to put too many colors on a bed; stick to white as the background color.

A guest room should be free of your clutter, hotel-like but with your personal touches, giving guests the luxury of peace within a friend's home. Don't use the guest room closet to store old clothes; that is such a turn-off when staying with someone.

CREATING A WELCOMING GUEST ROOM

Remove all old magazines and replace with current issues.

Put yourself in your guest's place and give the room those little touches that would make you feel important and welcome in your home.

Leave the room as neutral as possible, even putting away your personal photos when someone is visiting.

If you can, include a luggage rack like hotels have.

Feature a favorite heirloom or other piece of furniture. Your guests will enjoy getting to know you as you tell them why it is precious to you.

Bathrooms have high traffic and are often neglected when it comes to decorating. Next to the bedrooms, the bathrooms are the most personal rooms in the house and should be treated as such. The bathroom is one of the most costly rooms to build and remodel. As we know, when remodeling a home it is always wise to put money into the kitchen and bathrooms.

BATHROOMS
WASHROOMS AND POWDER ROOMS

As in the kitchen, my preference is to have pieces of furniture rather than built-ins, to create a cozy, country feel. Decorating with family photographs, fresh piles of tiles or even just one lone flower makes a bathroom inviting—especially to guests. It gives them a sense that the bathroom has not been neglected.

I avoid clutter at any cost.

Bathrooms can so easily begin to overflow with odds and ends. When building a bathroom from scratch or remodeling, I like to install a pony wall to hide the loo, and if there is room, an old armoire or chest of drawers to house all the toiletries.

When the kids were little, they would read to me from the upholstered chair while I took baths. Or the other way round. Nothing is better than a relaxing bath. (Note the small blocks below each claw; the old tub was so heavy we had to reinforce the floor.)

We all tear out magazine pages showing favorite room ideas. These a very useful tools to help a decorator get ideas and feelings of how you want your home to look. One of the first tasks I ask of a new client is to go through a well-edited binder of tear sheets using sticky notes to inform me not only what she likes but also what she doesn't like.

Many of the houses I've worked on have given me inspiration for other projects. In particular, the bathroom in this Connecticut farmhouse, where I spent time while working with the client on fabric choices, presented some ideas that I have borrowed for other projects: for instance, placing a comfortable but functional chair in the bathroom makes a handy place for tossing clothing or for sitting while putting on stockings or lavishing one's legs with lotion. And who doesn't like to read in the bathroom?

Illustrated are three takes on Roman shades.for a bathroom. A decorative Roman shade can be pulled down at night, while a sheer lining provides privacy throughout the day.

LEFT TO RIGHT : vintage with plain sheer; "Paisley" with red striped sheer; "George" red stripe with white sheer.

To naturally create ambiance

in a room, it's important to remember the interplay of color
and light especially through the use of fabric.

—Fiona Lewis

For this house in south-
ern France, an old tool
shed was turned into a
bathroom for the guest-
house. The French doors
lead out to the swimming
pool, so it doubles as a
changing room. Leftover
mosaic tiles from the pool
were glued onto the back-
splash. I'm always on the
lookout for ways to use
leftover bits and pieces. I
hate wastefulness.

ORDER AND

In towels, as with linens,

CLEANLINESS ARE

white rules the day. Colored towels

KEY. TOO MUCH

trying to match rugs are

STORAGE MEANS

too self-conscious,

HOARDING.

Never let a room look decorated.

Your idea, Kathryn,

of using fabric in the tiny powder room was incredible. It was cozy, warm, yet cheerful and intimate. With dimmer lights and a teeny-tiny window, the room was delicious.

—Serena McCallum

Something old and something new. A house can dictate how you live in it.

FACING: I used a modern-style bowl sitting on top of the original stone sink that was impractical for use as a sink today.

ABOVE: This old pine dresser belongs to my client's family and they wanted to somehow use it in their new home. We adapted it to hold the wash-basin in this powder room and fitted it with an antique brass bowl and taps.

This bathroom almost feels like a second bedroom. The wide-open space, the wood floors and the centrally placed tub all work together to create one of the most relaxing spaces in the house.

This well-proportion Connecticut bathroom was originally a bedroom, but when renovating the house, my client saw the importance of having a large bathroom that included a fire-place (unseen). The color scheme here is modest: different shades of brown wood, white porcelain and walls, pastel accent on the baseboards and in the flooring, and a big splash of color at the windows.

Kathryn's fabrics

make me feel like I'm on holiday.

—Rebecca Pigeon

When designing my collection of textiles for the home, I started off with prints and, as the collection evolved, added wovens. It had always been difficult to find a very simple sheer that also had some interest to it. This Belgium linen, woven with a vertical stripe of solid threads to add just a touch of color where needed, has been the perfect solution. It looks white until you get close up, and then the colored stripes lend just a bit of surprise.

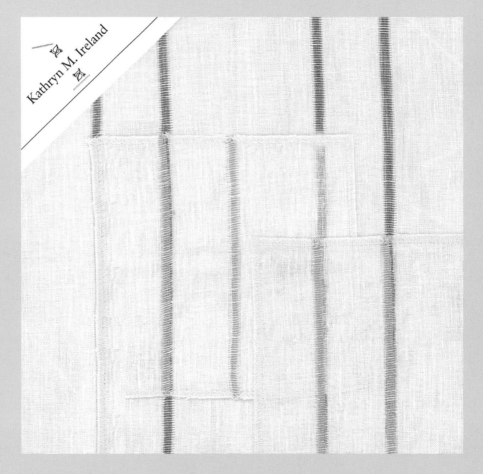

Kathryn M. Ireland

K athryn's sense of proportions, color and realism for our lifestyles make her rooms feel alive, inviting and livable. The best compliment of all is when a guest says it doesn't feel like a decorator has decorated.

—Kari Lyn Sabin-Jones

lighting is a major consideration in a bathroom. A combination of overhead and wall-mounted fixtures are ideal, as together they create flattering, soft light. Dimmers are essential.

Space permitting, a piece of soft furnishing to sit on or toss clothes onto is very useful. This cloverleaf-shaped ottoman makes a perfect center- piece in this room. Seamless glass shower walls add a touch of modernity to this otherwise vintage-looking space.

Bathrooms should carry the same look and feel as the rest of the house. Free and clean, the utilitarian look has made way for this room to be as important as any other room.

☒ Use freestanding furniture pieces—not too many built-ins. This will give your bathroom a comfortable country look while providing just enough storage space for essentials. Personally, I dislike having a lot of storage space, as it means hoarding more stuff. I like having only what I use; otherwise I end up with out-of-date lotions that just gather dust.

☒ Your bathroom is often a place where guests don't go, so you can let the room reflect who you are. This is a good place to display your very personal pictures and belongings. I always put up pictures in frames and decorate with things that feel like mine.

DECORATING DO'S FOR BATHROOMS

☒ Use your old trophies from earlier sports days to hold makeup pencils and brushes. I don't like things to be just ornamental; everything in my house has been adapted for everyday use.

☒ A traditional claw-foot tub is much more attractive than one that is built in. With this product available new on the market, schlepping home an antique bathtub and paying a small fortune to refurbish it is a thing of the past. Waterworks has done for bathrooms what Farrow & Ball has done for paint. Just as the value of an English house was raised by having an Aga in the kitchen, so too has the American bath-room by having Waterworks plumbing.

☒ Let kids' bathrooms, especially, be fun. My son's bathroom is wallpapered in Kath Kidson's toothpaste and towel motif, while the light fixture is a basketball hoop.

☒ Wallpaper or hand-paint the walls in a bath or powder room. Because they are generally small in square footage, bathrooms cost less to redo when you want a change.

OUTDOOR SPACES

I live half my life in the out-of-doors, entertaining and working—in both Santa Monica and the south of France. The veranda just off my dining room in Santa Monica is as much a part of the house as any other room. There are few sunny days that don't find me sitting and working at the big round table overlooking the pool. In France, every door leads to a different grouping of furniture, and I will often eat breakfast in one area, follow the sun to another for lunch and settle in another to watch the sunset.

Kathryn's eye for fabric goes

unsurpassed. With such an inventive talent for mixing patterns, colors and textures all in one room, she has earned the right to be called artist.

—Fran Drescher

One of my very first guests to my house in southern France was Fran. At the time, I had only gotten as far as renovating three bedrooms. Indoor furniture was scarce and outdoor furniture was nonexistent. Fran said, "The place is beautiful, the view is spectacular, but where is the patio furniture?" Until that moment I had happily sat under the oak tree on a blanket with an inflatable paddling pool, but together we drove to Toulouse, headed for Habit to find deck chairs and hammocks. The Albi and Montauban flea markets were where the old iron beds were purchased.

FACING: My much-photographed dogs, Greta and Gitana, lounging in the afternoon sun.

ABOVE: Fran in hammock with my son Otis.

OUTDOOR SPACES

I work here,

ARE AS MUCH

take meals with the boys

A PART OF

and entertain

THE HOUSE

throughout the year.

AS ANY ROOM.

Adding color and pattern

to the outdoors, Kathryn's fabrics create charming settings that are intimate and comfortable. The outdoor spaces feel like an extension of our home's interior.

—Nancy Newberg

ABOVE: The country-style pine table and wicker chairs give this loggia with arched portals a European rather than Brentwood, California feel.

FACING: The wicker theme continues in all of the different outdoor rooms. An exterior fireplace is the focal point of this interior courtyard.

Three different rooms from this house open onto this space, making it very much part of the house.

THIS

sun-shaded area was created using a custom-made iron frame covered with rush matting. It provides the perfect amount of shade during the summer months in Montclar de Quercy, France.

FACING AND ABOVE
A mixture of rattan and iron-and-wood picnic chairs make this gravel terrace ideal outdoor space for entertaining.

BELOW: Louise Fletcher and Sophia Beddow preparing for a dinner al fresco.

Chair $200

Plate $25

View Priceless

My favorite childhood
memories have been spent
here. Long lunches, dinners,
dancing and a lot of laughing.

—Oscar Weis

The beauty of old buildings that were
once used for either farm equipment
or animals is their proportion. In my
Dutch barn in France, this room, with
views that extend as far as the
Pyrenees, is quite breathtaking and
was chosen by *Elle Décor* as one of
the top hundred rooms in the world.
The simplicity of the painted outdoor
chairs, the utilitarian table made by a
local carpenter has hosted many dinners and lunches over the years and
has doubled as an art studio for all
ages.

Tents are a great way to bring your friends and family together for an afternoon or evening of entertaining by bringing the indoors outside.

—Blythe Danner

Having been burned out with show houses, I agreed to do this Brentwood house on the condition that it wouldn't be too time-consuming, as I was leaving for my annual summer trip to France. Between getting Blythe Danner to be my muse and finding an old Indian wedding tent that had been collecting dust for some time in the attic, the resulting outdoor space was a hit.

Tenting an area of your outdoor space is a unique way to create a completely different feel for a special occasion at home. In this Moorish-inspired tent, large floor pillows, and low tables and stools covered in a variety of patterns and colors add interest at eye level and complement the brightly colored tent ceiling.

Growing up with vibrant colors and great landscaping has given me an eye for
my surroundings.

—Otis Weis

The colors from an old striped hammock gave inspiration to my outdoor collection. Oversized pillows serve as additional seating for both interior and exterior spaces.

CREATE YOUR OWN SPACE ANYWHERE

These beach umbrellas and carpet with folding beach chairs and table make an instant room. Whether at the beach, in your front yard or at a soccer game, you can create your own comfortable space with very few items. (Sanibel Island, Florida)

This pattern was inspired by wall etchings seen on a trip to Rajastan, India, and is named "Aloy" after one of my best friends.

Kathryn gave me exactly what I wanted: color, color and more color.

—John Ceriale

A selection of outdoor fabric used on custom-made furniture at Sanibel Island, Florida.

Outdoor spaces should feel like extensions of the home. Whether you live in the city and have just a small terrace or a balcony, or in fact have a garden—having some sense of connection to the natural world around you is important in a balanced living space.

❧ Use furniture that would make as much sense indoors as it does outdoors and create living room–like furniture groupings.

❧ Cover the furniture in fabrics as much as possible: cushions or slipcovers for the chairs, colorful cloths on the tables. I love color and pattern.

❧ The best chairs are ones that feel at home both indoors and out, that can be moved around from one area to another.

IDEAS FOR MAKING THE OUTDOORS PART OF YOUR HOME

❧ Plenty of pillows made of outdoor fabrics are multipurpose accessories. And here's another tip: outdoor fabric is also great for the kitchen; its durable, water-resistant finish handles all the kids' spillings without causing a fuss.

❧ Having flowers just outside your windows, whether in pots or boxes or in the ground, is beautiful and relaxing if you can manage it. Short of fabric, flowers are the best way to frame a window. My all-time favorites are climbing roses, cascading geraniums and lavender; all are simple to grow and easy to maintain in warmer climates.

❧ Don't be too formal; having good-looking furniture is fine for outside, but you should feel comfortable and relaxed first and foremost.

FABRIC SOURCES Colors listed from back to front

Page 31
Kathryn Ireland
"Quilt,"
Butterscotch

Kathryn Ireland
"Scroll,"
Tomato/Butter

Kathryn Ireland
"Papoose,"
Butter/Tomato

Page 35
Kathryn Ireland
"Quilt," Red

Rogers & Goffigon
"Country Cloth
Plain," Borax

Kathryn Ireland
"Oscar," Red

Page 45
Chelsea Textiles

Kathryn Ireland
"Woven," Green

Kathryn Ireland
"Woven," Blue

Page 53
Kathryn Ireland
"Tulip," Pink

Kathryn Ireland
"Ikat Stripe,"
Red

Kathryn Ireland
"Ogee," Multi

Page 55
Kathryn Ireland
"Sheer," Yellow

Kathryn Ireland
"Roses," Red

Page 65
Kathryn Ireland
"Floral Jacquard,"
Natural

Kathryn Ireland
"Claude"

Kathryn Ireland
"Woven," Tan

Chelsea Textiles
"Vines and
Flowers"

Page 67
Robert Kime
Claremont

Kathryn Ireland
"Sheer Stripe,"
Tan

Page 69
Calvin Fabrics
"Salvage Silk
Croissant"

Kathryn Ireland
"George," Red

Kathryn Ireland
"George," Green

Page 70
De La Cuona

Rogers & Goffigon
"Wool Velvet,"
Mutzu

Kathryn Ireland
"George," Green

Rogers & Goffigon
"Cashmere," Tan

Clarence House

Page 72
Kathryn Ireland
"Quilt," Pug

Kathryn Ireland
"Greta," Blue

Rogers & Goffigon
"Barksdale
Roman 2," Loire

Page 75
Kathryn Ireland
"Claude," Chester

Kathryn Ireland
"Greta," Chester

Kathryn Ireland
"Floral Jacquard,"
Natural

Page 77
Kathryn Ireland
"Quilt,"
Butterscotch

Kathryn Ireland
"Woven," Tan

Kathryn Ireland
"Oscar,"
Butterscotch

PAGE 83

Robert Kime
"Indian Pear"

Kathryn Ireland
"Storybook,"
Silver Tree

PAGE 85

Rogers & Goffigon
"Cyclades,"
Andros

Kathryn Ireland
"Woven," Green

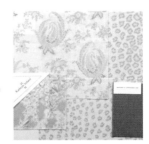

PAGE 86

Cowtan & Tout
"Livingston"

Kathryn Ireland
"Paisley Striped,"
Tan

Kathryn Ireland
"Ikat," Tan

Rogers & Goffigon
"Teddy," Tabac

PAGE 89

Bennison Fabrics
"Tokyo Rose,"
Faded Tan

Kathryn Ireland
"Large Ikat
Check,"
Firehouse

Cowtan & Tout
"Montauk Stripe"

S. Harris

PAGE 91

Robert Kime
"Alvedon"

Kathryn Ireland
"Ribbed," Silver
Tree

Rogers & Goffigon
"Teddy," Tabac

Kathryn Ireland
"Woven," Red

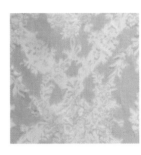

PAGE 100

Kathryn Ireland
Yellow

Ottoman fabric
not shown here

Bennison
"Faded Rose"

PAGE 113 (counter-
clockwise from upper
left)

Oscar de la Renta

Pacifica Hide
"Leather"

Promenade
Black Cherry

Robert Kime
"Turkeman Stripe"

Kathryn Ireland
"Woven," Yellow

PAGE 122

Chelsea Textiles
"Jungle Crewel
Work"

Kathryn Ireland
"Tulip," Red

Kathryn Ireland
"Toile," Red

Raoul Textiles
"Cunari," Red

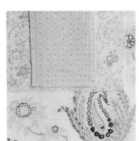

PAGE 127

Kathryn Ireland
"Paisley Striped,"
Red

Kathryn Ireland
"Floral," Green

Kathryn Ireland
"Tonal Ticking,"
Yellow

PAGE 132

Bennison
"Orchid Lilly"

Kathryn Ireland
"Floral," Red

PAGE 135

Kathryn Ireland
"Paisley Stripe,"
Pink

Kathryn Ireland
"Two-Toned
Ticking," Pink

Kathryn Ireland
"Floral," Pink

PAGE 136

Kathryn Ireland
"Roses," Pink

Kathryn Ireland
"Tonal Ticking,"
Pink

Page 138

Cowtan & Tout
"New World"

Kathryn Ireland
"Tonal Ticking,"
Blue

Osborne & Little

Kathryn Ireland
"George," Red

Osborne & Little

Page 142

Kathryn Ireland
"Ikat," Green

Kathryn Ireland
"Quilt," Pink

Kathryn Ireland
"Floral," Green

Page 147

Kathryn Ireland
"Large Ikat
Check"

Kathryn Ireland
"Toile," Red

Kathryn Ireland
"Ribbed," Red

Kathryn Ireland
"Sheer," White

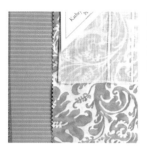

Page 153

Gretchen Bellinger

Fortuny

Kathryn Ireland
"Sheer Stripe,"
White

Page 154

Raoul Textiles
"Mahatma"

Kathryn Ireland
"Small Check,"
Blue

Kathryn Ireland
"Floral," Blue

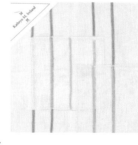

Page 158

Kathryn Ireland
"Ikat," Blue

Kathryn Ireland
"Floral," Blue

Kathryn Ireland
"Ribbed," Silver
Tree

Page 164

Kathryn Ireland
"Ikat Stripe,"
Firehouse

Peter Dunham

Kathryn Ireland
"Woven," Red

Le Gracieux

Page 167

Ralph Lauren
"Seersucker,"
Blue

Kathryn Ireland
"Paisley Striped,"
Indigo

Kathryn Ireland
"Greta," Indigo

Page 188

Kathryn Ireland
"Sheer Stripe,"
Blue

Kathryn Ireland
"Sheer Stripe,"
Yellow

Kathryn Ireland
"Sheer Stripe,"
Pink

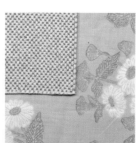

Page 203

Kathryn Ireland
"Floral Batik,"
Yellow

Kathryn Ireland
"Boucle," Blue

Page 190

Rose Tarlow

Kathryn Ireland
"Sheer," Green

Page 192

Kathryn Ireland
"Toile," Red

Kathryn Ireland
"Sheer," White

Page 215

Kathryn Ireland
Outdoor Collection
"Abu," Yellow
"Abu," Orange
"Stripe," Multi
"Abu," Green
"Abu," Turquoise

ACKNOWLEDGMENTS

TO MY FRIENDS AND CLIENTS who were generous enough to let me include their homes in this book:

Leah Adler	Steve Martin
Julia Louis-Dreyfus and Brad Hall	Serena McCallum
Peter Dunham	Ann McNally
Louise Fletcher	Bruce and Nancy Newburg
Lady Annabel Goldsmith	David Mamet and Rebecca Pigeon
Kate and Ben Goldsmith	Andy Sabin
Ann and Keith Halsey	Kari Lyn Sabin-Jones
The Honorable Katherine Hesketh	Windsor Smith
James Holland Hibbert	Victoria Tenant
Leslie and Mark Johnson	

To all the magazine editors who have supported me over the years. in particular, Margaret Russell, *Elle Décor*; Domenique Browning, *House and Gardens*; Stephen Drucker, *House Beautiful*; Rupert Thomas, *World of Interiors*; Sue Crew, *House and Gardens*, UK.

To everyone in the trade, at whom I'm sure I've screamed and yelled at some point in their lives.

Jackie Terrell for her illustrations.

Susan Maltby, who came here to primal scream and found her true calling with a needle and thread.

Dulce, Wendy and Anna Deleon.

Carol Ross and Joe Rigoli for keeping me on the straight and narrow.

To my friends and family who've put up with those summers in France.

To Jan Scott for coming in and out of my life as needed.

To Gibbs Smith and especially Madge Baird, whose ideas are always better than mine.

And lastly, to Oscar, Otis and Louis, who've posed for endless photos and for being mere accessories and inspiration to my success.

PHOTO CREDITS

Alexander Bailhache
Page 151 (bottom left)

Tim Beddows
Pages 6, 12, 14, 20, 23 (top right) 28, 29 (top right), 30, 31(top right), 34, 37 (bottom right), 36, 40, 42–48, 52–53 (top left), 54, 56, 60–64, 66–95, 96, 103–104 (left), 106–116, 120–123, 126–127 (bottom), 130–135, 138–145, 148–150, 151 (right)–159, 160 (top right/bottom right), 161–163, 168, 172–179, 180–181 (right), 183–192, 196, 202–205 (top), 206 (top), 212, 214–215, Back Cover (far left and right)

Cindy Gold
Pages 166–167,

Grey Crawford
Page 208–209 (top left and right)

Henry Bourne/*Elle Décor*
Cover, Pages. 2, 4, 22, 24, 25 (top right), 128–129, 160 (far left), 198, 207

Francoise Halard
Pages 23 (bottom right), 102, 124, 210, 216, Back Cover (middle)

Oberto Gili
Pages 32, 50–51, 105, 136–137, 147, 165

Dominique Vorillon
Pages 18, 21, 26

Michael Miller
All fabric swatches and Pages. 8, 35 (lower right), 211 (top and bottom left), 218–220; Back Flap

Tim Street Porter
Pages 201

RESOURCES

KATHRYN IRELAND SHOWROOMS

ANN DENNIS
2915 Redhill Ave., Suite B106-7
Costa Mesa, CA 92626
714.708.2555 • Fax: 714.708.2554

COUNTRY GEAR
PO Box 727
2408 Main St.
Bridgehampton, NY 11932
631.537.7069 • Fax: 631.537.6979

DORIAN BAHR COMPANIES
Decorative Center Houston
5120 Woodway Dr., Suite 130
Houston, TX 77056
713.599.0900 • Fax: 713.599.0905

ELINOR AND VERVE
5601 6th Ave. South
Showroom 268
Seattle, WA 98108
206.767.6941 • Fax: 206.767.7011

GRIZZEL & MANN
351 Peachtree Hills Ave., Suite 120
Atlanta, GA 30305
404.261.5932 • Fax: 404.261.5958

ID COLLECTION
1025 Stemmons Fwy., Suite 745
Dallas, TX 75207
214.698.0226 • Fax: 214.698.8650

INTO
40 N. Hotel St.
Honolulu, HI 96813
808.536.2211 • Fax: 808.536.2266

JOHN ROSSELLI & ASSOCIATES
D&D Building
979 Third Ave., Suite 701
New York, NY 10022
212.593.2060 • Fax: 212.832.3687

JOHN ROSSELLI & ASSOCIATES
1515 Wisconsin Ave., NW
Washington, DC 20007
202.337.7676 • Fax: 202.337.4443

Design Center of the Americas
1855 Griffin Rd., Suite A-128
Dania, FL 33004
954.920.1700 • Fax: 954.920.5686

6-158 Merchandise Mart
Chicago, IL 60654
312.822.0760 • Fax: 312.822.0764

JOHN BROOKS
601 S. Broadway, Suite L
Denver, CO 80209
303.698.9977 • Fax: 303.698.9797

2732 N. 68th St., Suite 1
Scottsdale, AZ 85257
480.675.8828 • Fax: 480.675.7722

KATHRYN IRELAND
Fairbanks Studio 2
65-69 Lots Road
London, England SW10 0RN
020.7751.4554 • Fax: 020.7751.4555

MACARENA SAIZ
Velazquez, 115 bajo-5
Madrid 28006, Spain
34.915.62.47.54 • Fax: 34.914.1115.84

MAVROMAC (PTY) LTD.
PO Box 76178
Wendywood 2144
South Africa
01127.444.1584 • Fax: 01127.444.1541

BARBARA MOREIRA
Av. Montevideu 236
4150 Porto, Portugal
351.22.6163806 • Fax: 351.22.6163808

ROOMS & GARDENS
924 State St.
Santa Barbara, CA 93101
805.965.2424 • Fax: 805.965.2755

1311 Montana Ave.
Santa Monica, CA 90402
310.451.5154 • Fax: 310.319.3485

SHELLEY CHOPARD
34 O'Niel St.
Lilyfield, Australia NSW2040
61.438.897.823

ROAD REP-LOS ANGELES
Nicky Rising
310.560.5027 • Fax: 818.766.1932

ANTIQUES, FURNITURE AND LIGHTING

ADESSO
38 E. Holly St.
Pasadena, CA 91103
626.683.3511
www.adessoimports.com

AGA RANGES, INC
110 Woodcrest Rd.
Cherry Hill, NJ 08003
866.424.2487
www.aga-ranges.com

ALFIE'S MARKET
13–25 Church St.
Marylebone
London NW8 8DT, UK.
020.7723.6066 • Fax: 020.7724.0999

AMY PERLIN ANTIQUES
306 E. 61st St.
New York, NY 10021
212.593.5756 • Fax: 212.593.5240

2462 Main Street
Bridgehampton, NY 11932
631.537.6161 • Fax: 631.537.6999

ANN MORRIS ANTIQUES, INC.
239 E. 60th Street
New York, NY 10022
212 755 3170 • Fax: 212 838 4955

ANTOINE & NOEMI
47 Rue du Chateau du Roi
Gaillac 81600, France
33.563.810.133

BELLA FIGURA LTD
Decoy Farm
Old Church Road
Melton, Suffolk IP13 6DH
(0)7000.235.523 • Fax: (0)7000.235.524

BLANCHARD
86/88 Pimlico Rd.
London SW7W8PL, UK.
020 78236310

BOURGET BROS.
1636 11th St.
Santa Monica, CA 90404
310.450.6556

BOURGET FLAGSTONE COMPANY
1810 Colorado Blvd.
Santa Monica, CA 90404
310.829.4010

CHRISTOPHER FARR RUGS
Ground Floor 6 Burnsall St.
London SW3 3ST, UK.
020.7349.0888 • Fax: 020.7349.0088

COUNTRY GEAR, LTD.
2408 Main Street
PO Box 727
Bridgehampton, NY 11932
631.537.7069
www.loom-italia-usa.com

CRATE AND BARREL
Customer Service Department
1860 W. Jefferson Ave.
Naperville, IL 60540
800.967.6696
www.crateandbarrel.com

DESIGN WITHIN REACH
225 Bush St., 20th Floor
San Francisco, CA 94104
1.800.944.2233
www.dwr.com

ECCOLA
326 N. La Brea Ave.
Los Angeles, CA 90036
323.932.9922
www.eccolaimports.com

ELSON RUGS
800.944.2858
www.elsoncompany.com

FARROW & BALL
1054 Yonge St.
Toronto, ON
888.511.1121
www.farrow-ball.com

GEORGE SMITH
587–589 Kings Rd.
London SW6 2EH, UK.
020.7384.1004 • Fax: 020.7731.4451
www.gsmithdata.co.uk

GEORGE TERBOVICH DESIGN INC
315 E. 55th St.
Kansas City, MO 64113
816.361.2100

GLOSTER FURNITURE LIMITED
Collins Drive, Severn Beach
Bristol BS35 4GG, UK.
014.5463.1950 • Fax: 014.5463.1959
Catalog Request Line: 014.5463.1955
uk@gloster.com

HABITAT
42–46 Princelet St.
London E1 5LP, UK.
020.7428.1771
www.habitat.net

HAZLITT HOLLAND HIBBERT:
Dealers in modern painting, drawing and
sculpture

LONDON
38 Bury St.
St James's, London SW1Y 6BB, UK.
020.7839.7600 • Fax: 020.7839.7255

NEW YORK
17 E. 76th St.
New York, NY 10021
212.772.1950 • Fax: 212.772.9402

HOLLYHOCK
817 Hilldale Ave.
West Hollywood, CA 90069
310.777.0100
www.hollyhockinc.com

JANUS & CIE
8687 Melrose Ave., Space 146
Los Angeles, CA 90069
310.652.7090
www.janusetcie.com

JEWEL BOX
3100 Wilshire Blvd.
Santa Monica, CA 90403
310.828.6900
www.jewelboxframes.com

JOHN ROSSELLI INTERNATIONAL
523 E. 73rd St.
New York, NY 10021
212.772.2137 • Fax: 212.535.2989
www.johnrosselliantiques.com

KATHRYN M IRELAND STUDIO
1619 Stanford St.
Santa Monica, CA 90404
310.315.4351

LIEF ANTIQUES
646 N. Almont
West Hollywood, CA 90069
310.492.0033

LOUISE FLETCHER
1520 S. Campe Ave.
Los Angeles, CA 90025
310.477.5049
lfdp2@aol.com

MCCAFFREY ROSEMARIE ANTIQUES
1203 Montana Ave.
Santa Monica, CA 90403
310.395.7711

MCKINNEY & CO
Studio P The Old Imperial Laundry
71 Warriner Gardens
Battersea, London SW11 4XW, UK
020.7627.5077
www.mckinney.co.ok/

NATHAN TURNER ANTIQUES
636 Almont Dr.
Los Angeles, CA 90069
310.275.1209
www.nathanturner.com

NIGEL WAYMOUTH
213.891.1919
www.nigelwaymouth.com

PETER FETTERMAN PHOTOGRAPHY
Bergamot Station
2525 Michigan Ave., Gallery A7
Santa Monica, CA 90404
310.453.6463 • Fax: 310.453.6959

POTTERY BARN INC. HEADQUARTERS
3250 Van Ness Ave.
San Francisco, CA 94109
415.421.7900
www.potterybarn.com

ROBERT KIME
121–121A
Kensington Church Street
London W8 2LP UK
020.7229.0886

ROBERT A. M. STERN ARCHITECTS LLP
460 W. 34th St.
New York, NY 10001
212.967.5100
www.ramsa.com

SAG HARBOR ANTIQUES
PO Box 1500
Sag Harbor, NY 11963
516.725.1732

SHABBY CHIC
RACHEL ASHWELL DESIGNS, INC.
6330 Arizona Cr.
Los Angeles, CA 90045
310.258.0660 • Fax: 310.258.0661

TALISMAN
79–91 New Kings Rd.
London SW6 4SQ, UK.
020.7731.4686 • Fax: 020.7731.0444

TOWN & COUNTRY
476 Mac Curtain Street
Cork, Ireland
353.21.501468

VAUGHAN DESIGNS INC
D & D Building
979 Third Ave., Suite 1511
New York, NY 10022
212.319.7070 • Fax: 212.319.7766

VAUGHAN LIMITED
G1, Chelsea Harbour Design Center
Chelsea Harbour
London SW 10 0XE, UK.
UK Sales: 020.7349.4600
Export Sales: 020.7349.4601
Fax: 020.7349.4615

VALERIE WADE
108 Fulham Rd.
London SW3 6HS, UK.
020.7225.1414 • Fax: 020.7589.9029

WATERWORKS
60 Backus Ave.
Danbury, CT 06810
800.927.2120
www.waterworks.com

WESTENHOLZ ANTIQUES LTD.
76–78 Pimlico Rd.
London, England SW1W 8PL
020.7824.8090
www.westenholz.co.uk

FABRICS

GRETCHEN BELLINGER
24 Mill St.
Albany, NY 12204
518.445.2400 • Fax: 518.445.1200
www.gretchenbellinger.com

BENNISON FABRICS INC
232 E. 59th St.
New York, NY 10022
212.223.0373
www.bennisonfabrics.com

CHELSEA TEXTILES
979 Third Ave.
New York, NY 10022
212.319.5804
www.chelseatextiles.com

CLAREMONT FURNISHING
FABRICS COMPANY
35, Elystan St.
London SW3 3NT, UK.
020.7581.9575 • Fax: 020.7581.9573
www.claremontfurnishing.com

COWTAN & TOUT
111 8th Ave., Suite 9630
New York, NY 10011
212.647.6901

DE LE CUONA DESIGNS LTD.
1 Trinity Place
Windsor, Berkshire SL4 3 3AP, UK.
017.5383.0301

PETER DUNHAM
909 N. Orlando Ave.
Los Angeles, CA 90069
323.848.7799
www.peterdunham.com

FORTUNY
979 Third Ave., Suite 1632
New York, NY 10022
www.fortuny.com

HENRY CALVIN FABRICS
2046 Lars Way
Medford, OR 97501
541.732.1996
www.henrycalvin.com

NINA CAMPBELL
9 Walton St.
London SW3 2JD, UK.
020.7225.1011 • Fax: 020.7225.0644
www.ninacampbell.com

OSBORNE & LITTLE
8687 Melrose Ave., B643
West Hollywood, CA 90069
310.659.7667
www.osborneandlittle.com

OSCAR DE LA RENTA LTD
550 7th Ave.
New York, NY 10018
212.282.0500
www.oscardelarenta.com

PACIFIC HIDE & LEATHER
3260 E. 59th St.
Long Beach, CA 90805
800.472.4567
www.pacifichide.com

RAOUL TEXTILES
110 Los Aguajes Ave.
Santa Barbara, CA 93101
805.965.1694 • Fax: 805.965.0907
www.raoultextiles.com

ROGERS & GOFFIGON LTD
41 Chestnut St.
Greenwich, CT 06830
203.532.8068

ROBERT KIME
PO Box 454
Marlborough, Wiltshire SN8 3UR, UK.
020.7229.0886
www.robertkime.com

S. HARRIS & CO
8687 Melrose Ave.
Los Angeles, CA 90069
310.358.0404

SILK TRADING COMPANY
360 S. La Brea
Los Angeles, CA 90036
323.954.9280
www.silktrading.com

ROSE TARLOW MELROSE HOUSE
8454 Melrose Place
Los Angeles, CA 90069
323.651.2202
www.rosetarlow.com

NATHAN TURNER
636 N. Almont Dr.
Los Angeles, CA 90069
310.275.1209
www.nathanturner.com